W0006230

Widgivation

By: Widgi Marcelin

Dedications:

I dedicate this book to everyone who wants to do better in life.

I dedicate this book to everyone who comes from where I come from and overcame the struggle or who is ready to overcome it.

Acknowledgements:

I would like to first thank God for helping me through the trials and tribulations. My family and friends who have supported everything I do and my publisher for helping me bring my vison to life.

Introduction

I wrote this book to inspire. I came from Haiti, a third-world country, and from poverty. I turned my life around despite everything I had experienced. This book gives people hope despite any circumstance or battle they may face. If I can do it, so can you. I want to provide a little background of who I am, where I came from, and how I began my journey in the USA. Growing up in Haiti wasn't easy, but my family made do with the resources we were given. I was always a leader, my siblings looked up to me, and I don't say that lightly or arrogantly. My mother knew I would be something special, especially after 3 days of labor. It took me a while to come into this world because God took his time. Where I grew up, it wasn't safe; the chaos, the crime, and the government all played a part in the horrendous environment. Although we lived in these conditions, my mother did her best to support and care for me.

During that era, I couldn't say it was all bad because I wasn't used to anything else. This was home, and all I knew. I spent my days playing on the dirt roads, going to school, and spending a lot of time alone. If you ask my mother, she will tell you I was mischievous, always telling a joke to see others smile, but I was also a loner. Going off and doing my own thing wasn't uncommon for me. I was always in my thoughts; I was always daydreaming about becoming bigger and better, and sometimes being better meant that I would have to leave all that I knew and the most important woman in my life behind. That time came when the nature of Haiti caused me to leave. Everyone's safety was jeopardized due to asylum. An asylum This means refugees would leave their country due to feeling unsafe because of the persecution they have suffered. Or may suffer because of race, religion, or other factors. Because of this, I made my way to Palm Beach, Florida, at 12. During my time here, I've made mistakes, endured trials and tribulations, been in jail, and been shot. This list goes on, but there's a light in every dark tunnel. I aim for this book to be the light at the end of your tunnel. Even in your darkest hour, you remember the words, quotes, and lessons I've given you to keep going. Hard times don't last forever.

.

I suggest you stay positive and speak positively.

It will always bring the best results.

One thing we can all agree on is that life is difficult at times. Life can hit you with more curve balls, twists, and turns than we would ever imagine. I won't lie and say that it's easy to remain positive or speak life into yourself because when life hits, it is most likely when you least expect it. But what I will say is that it's mandatory to watch our thoughts. Our thoughts and tongue will shape our future, past, and present if you think that you have bad luck, that's surely what you will have. If you sink into depression and think you'll never come out of that, you won't. Our thoughts are our reality. This exercise helped me change my mindset when I thought nothing was going right.

I set the alarm on my phone to say 3 things I am thankful for. Some days all I said was that I was grateful for was breath in my body. But it was something. I did this for 21 days straight until my mind was programmed only to focus on what I was thankful for versus what I lacked. Once you do this, the things you lack will become what you have. It's like a switch in our brain that can identify with positivity and produce positive results. Once you see those results, remember to remain humble and thankful. Anything given can always be taken away. This also ties into manifestation. Our thoughts and tongue are pivots when manifesting the life we deserve or desire to live. It's as simple as writing down your goals and checking them off. This keeps our thoughts positive on what we want, and writing them will help our subconscious mind stay focused for the best results.

CREATE SOME POSITIVE AFFIRMATIONS TO SPEAK DAILY.

If you don't program yourself, life will program you.

Every day I suggest you have a positive start or program for how your morning will go. The way you start your day pivots to how it will end. If your day starts in chaos, sometimes it will end that way. This isn't to say a bad morning can't be turned around. However, it is more likely to be positive and remain that way if that's the start. Here is a sample of a routine I do every morning. After I wake up and take care of my hygiene, I meditate and pray for at least 5 minutes. I then answer any business emails, texts, or calls from the night before. After I take care of business, I decide on my outfit, shoes, and jewelry, and then I start my day.

Most days, people get on social media immediately after waking up. Before they thank God or even check on their kids. I am not judging anyone, but I believe starting your day with prayer and meditation can change a lot. When I say life will program you, I mean that life will give you any ole thing and say, "here, it's yours." You are way better than getting handed anything. Do not let life program you because instead of standing out like you were born to do, you will blend in. You'll agree with the latest trends, hairstyles, and lingo; before you know it, you've lost sight of who you are. It's very important to remain authentic, especially in this generation. Get on a program that fits you, and stay true to yourself while doing it.

LIST YOUR MORNING ROUTINE.

I used to be ungrateful for not always having more.

Until I lost it all.

Don't be the old me; appreciate every blessing daily.

One thing I saw when I came to America was how much we complained about what we didn't have. Remembering life in Haiti made me understand that the little things count. We have to understand the privilege we have in the US. My country didn't even have electricity every night, let alone cable TV. We get caught up in the luxuries of life and forget to thank God for the little things. We fail to thank God for the legs we have to get out of bed every day. There's someone who would love your legs. Or even our heart beats just right because someone is wearing a heart monitor. It's the small things that we have to be thankful for to be blessed with more.

Growing up, there weren't any Gucci, Cartier watches or diamond grills. We had dirt roads, the food we put together, and the houses we shared. The house you may be in may not be your dream home, but it's a roof over your head. I can't bet my last dollar that a person in Haiti or even Skid Row in LA would love the house you're in. That car may not be the best but guess what? It gets you where you need to go. God blesses those who are thankful for what they have currently because how will you appreciate what's to come if you don't? Every tunnel has a light;

sometimes, we must go to the dark and enjoy it first.

WHAT ARE YOU GRATEFUL FOR?

You must love yourself, talk to yourself, and compliment yourself.

Today's era is different from where many of us grew up in. There weren't social media to tell us how to look, what to wear, or how our bodies should look. This goes for men and women. A lot of people end their lives or become depressed on account of strangers—people who will never meet you or see you a day in their life. Many measure success and what it looks like based on strangers, again, people they will never meet. To live your life based on you and no one else, you must love yourself.

Once you love who you are, there is nothing anyone can say to depreciate that love. In addition to loving yourself, many people don't understand that no one else will if you don't love yourself properly. How can you accept someone loving you when you don't even love yourself? There is nothing wrong with changing your body, hair, or appearance. But before you do so, be sure to love who you are before the altering. Because after the altering, you'll find something else to be unhappy about, and you'll continue changing yourself based on strangers. Talk to yourself often. When I say talk, I mean speak kind words to yourself. If you constantly speak negatively about yourself, you will negatively perceive yourself.

It takes 22 days to create a habit that can stick for life. So, if I am talking badly to myself and putting myself down, my brain picks that up. Once my brain picks up, that's all I will ever think of myself. But if you speak love, then love for yourself will be what you feel. This quote is one of the most important to remember in this society. As for me, I don't compare myself to any rapper or businessman. I know who I am and where I am going, and I love every inch of me. There is not a rapper or man I want to be like. There is only one Widgi, and there will never be another like me.

As I said before, social media has altered reality. But who's to say social media's standards are right? You can't help how you were born; this is what God gave you. Embrace it, love it, love you, and don't worry about anything else. Be selfish with your self-love. There is only one of you.

WHAT DO YOU LOVE ABOUT YOURSELF
AND WHY?

What's stopping you from starting your business?

Start today.

I'll start tomorrow, next week, or Monday, which is what I hear when people talk about starting their dream business. 9 times out of 10, tomorrow, next week, or Monday will never come. When we procrastinate on our dreams, they never become a reality. A dream is only without action; it stays in our heads. You can have the best product in your mind, but the world will never know. Fear, anxiety, and lack of confidence keep us from fulfilling our life's purpose. It's okay to be nervous but do it nervous. Sometimes we feel that the market we are in is oversaturated. When that thought comes into your head, remember there are 14 plus bread companies in one bread aisle. Gucci, Dior, and Fendi all sell clothes, shoes, purses, and more. They sell the same product with a different logo and make millions.

You have to believe you can achieve the type of success you want. If I thought about how many people did what I do, far as rapping (which is a business) or any of my business endeavors, I wouldn't be successful. You have to have tunnel vision and stay focused. Start that business, and even when it's slow, keep going;

you never know which day you'll hit your first million. You never know who's

watching you. You never know who you will inspire on your way to the top.

WHAT IS YOUR DREAM BUSINESS OR CAREER? WHAT STEPS ARE YOU TAKING TO START YOUR BUSINESS OR DREAM CAREER?

Don't ever be envious of what someone has.

Your bigger blessing could be right around the corner.

Are you ready for it?

Not being envious of others is sometimes very hard for people to do. Sometimes we come down hard on ourselves because we see the cars, jewelry, money, and clothes other people have and think, why not me? We see the big houses and the fame and wonder why don't we have those things. This is very dangerous thinking. Why? Because if you are constantly focused on what other people have, how will you ever reach your fullest potential? It's essential to keep your eyes on your prize because if you aren't careful, someone can steal it. Imagine you are building this lifestyle, and then you come across someone on Instagram and immediately stop being grateful for what you got.

Not knowing that your blessing could be tomorrow. But are you even ready for it? We want, want, and don't get me wrong, I want more success too. However, you must be prepared for those blessings to pour in without blockages. By blockages, I mean your mind, soul, and heart. You can block your blessings by counting others. How can God know it's time unless you are applying pressure to your life? The great point is that you don't know how people got to where they are. Sometimes people idolize people who don't even own the things they post. How do you know that's their money, cars, or houses? We don't; therefore, we mind our business and focus on our money, cars, and assets. Be thankful for what you have, and get ready for more blessings to pour in. They are only coming when YOU are ready.

HOW WILL YOU FEEL WHEN YOUR BIGGEST BLESSING COMES?

Always remember don't cheat the process.
Stay self-motivated and dedicated to achieve success.

Cheating the process will never and it will only hurt you in the long run. Let's say we are baking a cake, and for it to bake faster, you leave out an ingredient. This ingredient also boosts flavor, but you don't know; you want the cake done more quickly. Once the cake is made, you taste it, and it's not how it usually tastes. You don't even like it. That's how life is. We must go through every step to build success without skipping a step. Those steps are what make success stay long-term. There is no proper rule book for success in business or anything.

You can take a million classes; however, your journey will never be the same. So, let's say you have a couple hundred in sales one day and none for a week. Do you quit? If you say yes, then think of this. What if the day you were about to receive your first thousand-dollar order? It could even be your first million-dollar order.

If you say no, then think of this, tomorrow could be the day you reach a million in sales. If you knew that tomorrow was the day, would you quit? I know the answer is no because I wouldn't. Success is not a treadmill; it isn't fast, and you can't speed it up to your liking. You must go through the burn, bad, and good days: the slow days and the fast ones to appreciate success when you get it. Plus, the journey is how you'll have a story to inspire your kids or those coming up behind you.

Sometimes it takes years to develop a successful brand or business. Nowadays, it looks like it can be done overnight. Anything worth having is worth working hard for and worth the wait. Tomorrow could be your million-dollar day. Don't give up.

HOW ARE YOU STAYING DEDICATED TO YOUR GOALS?

Make sure you talk about your blessings more than your problems.

Sometimes it can be hard not to talk about what we are going through. Often we feel we need to vent, need that ear to listen, or maybe we need that advice. We sometimes forget the blessings when we complain or vent too much about our problems. Focusing on what we don't have can be poison to our life. Please think about it like this. If we are always complaining about what is going wrong, how will we ever see when it's going right? An example: You have been complaining about not having a car. You finally save to get a car, but it's not your dream car.

The car may come with a few minor problems, and now you're frustrated, so you complain. I get it; you didn't want to fix these problems but let's break down the problem in this. At first, you prayed for a car, and then you got it. Instead of being thankful for it, you decided to complain about the minor issues that the car has. Would you rather walk in the hot sun or cold, or would you rather deal with minor problems and be thankful? I would pick being thankful. Everything isn't always going to be perfect, and God isn't always going to give you exactly what you want. But you will get what you need. You needed that car, so instead of complaining, thank God for the car because you could be walking. We must remind ourselves that whining does nothing for our future but keeps us back. When I didn't have a car, I didn't complain; I thanked God for having the legs to walk. When I got a car, and it wasn't my dream car, I thanked God for not having to walk. When I got my dream car, I thanked God for giving me a car with no problems. It's levels to live and be thankful at all levels.

WHAT HAVE YOU BEEN BLESSED WITH?
DOESN'T MATTER HOW OLD OR NEW,
TELL ME ABOUT IT.

Reset and refocus as many times as you need.

Life is hard, it's hard on our mental health, and it's hard on our bodies; as a black man, mental health is very important in our community right now. We must understand that taking a step back from things is okay. When you work day in and day out, you can easily become burned out, especially in today's society. Self-care isn't just for women; it is for everyone. Self-care is having that spa day you like, shopping, or playing video games. Whatever happiness and peace look like for you, that's what you do on a self-care day.

Every week should be one day you take for yourself to unwind. When I say that, I mean no work, no business, just you and whatever you like to do. When working a 9-5 or building a brand, you have to give your brain and body a break; taking off your body will take care of you. Often we get so burned out that we quit or leave our business behind because we are overworked, underpaid, and stressed out mentally.

For your body to run at a healthy pace to achieve what you desire, you must rest, relax and refocus again. You must treat yourself with love and respect. Success isn't just about working the hardest or long sleepless nights. It's also about taking care of yourself first so that when you succeed, you aren't so overworked that you don't know how to enjoy it. There's nothing wrong with rest, don't rest too long you will forget what you want to achieve.

WRITE DOWN WHAT A SELF CARE DAY
LOOKS LIKE FOR YOU.

Always going out of your way for people can be why you miss out on your blessing.

This one is a hard lesson for some people, but I'm going to be the one to say it. Being a yes person always will make you tired, broke, and unhappy. This book is full of motivation, but it's also to help you out where you are possibly lacking in your daily life. Sometimes it's okay to help others; this is a fact that can bring blessings. However, when you are constantly that person who people can run to, not only are you taking losses but are they learning their lesson? You can't save everyone from everything. You are not responsible for people's shortcomings, failures, or blessings. Worry about you first and others later.

Nine times out of ten, you can give your last to someone, and they wouldn't give you a red cent. Here's an example: You are down to your last $250, and your friend needs $125. You give it to them because you have a good heart, and they need it. A few months later, your car breaks down, and you need $125, so you ask your friend to borrow the money. They don't even respond; they leave you on read. Where are these people who you help when you need help? Who saves the hero when they need to be saved? Sometimes, no one.

Don't let your heart trick you out of your blessings. We tend to believe everybody has to come to the top with us when we make money. This isn't true. The same friends you've had for years can turn into enemies over a green piece of paper. Everyone can't go on your journey, and you can block your blessings by allowing everyone to come. God will halt your blessings because these people don't deserve to come, aren't meant to come, or can hurt you in the long run. Everybody can't go, and you can't save everybody. Stop blocking your blessings from being a savior.

HOW CAN YOU SAY "NO" IN A RESPECTFUL WAY?

You must discipline yourself to achieve anything you want in life.

This is hard for some people because we live in a world where you must look at the part to be viewed in a certain light. Here's why it is harmful. Let's say you are saving for your business inventory. You have about $3,000 saved, but your friends invite you out to have fun. You don't have any extra money, but you have your inventory money and need an outfit. Instead of staying in, you buy a new outfit and drinks at the bar. Now your stash is $2,000. The next day your friends invite you on a road trip; although you know your goals, you need a new outfit to look the part, and you have to put money in for gas and a hotel, not to mention the sections at the club, food, and drinks. You don't have any extra money from paying bills, but you have $2,000 left from inventory. So, you take the $2,000 and have fun.

When you get home, you realize you have spent all your inventory money, and now you have to start all over. You did this for a 48-hour kick. Some might say live a little I will get it back. You could have missed out on the fun of funding your dreams. How will you achieve the goal if you jump on whenever something fun comes up? Sometimes we must sacrifice and understand that the outside isn't going anywhere. It will always be there when we finish our goals. The kick will always be around. The club, the clothes, and the trips will never die. But your goals can die right before your eyes. Do not waste your time and energy on things that serve you no purpose. Yes, we can have fun and spend money, but look at the bigger picture before you do.

Remember why you started saving in the first place. Real friends and family will understand. Sometimes you have to strip down from everything and go ghost. Then pop back out once you have completed everything. Making money is always going to be more important than spending it.

WHAT DO YOU NEED TO WORK ON?
WHAT ARE THE STEPS YOU ARE GOING
TO TAKE?

Take possession of your mind, and you may soon make life pay off on your terms.

Your mind is unquestionably your most valuable possession. You may lose every material you own, but knowledge can never be taken from you. With it, you can earn a new fortune, build a new home, and buy anything you truly desire. No one else can control your thoughts; even the cruelest tyrant cannot force you to think about something you refuse to accept. When you make a deliberate decision to take control of your mind and feed it positive, constructive thoughts, you are on your way to taking control of your life. The thoughts you allow to dominate your mind will determine what you will get from life. We must continue to remember what we think is our reality.

If your thoughts are poor, then it's sad to say so will you be. The mind is 80% of the reason we either have the success we want or the downfall we don't want. The thing about knowledge is that, in some cases, it's better than money itself. The knowledge you feed your mind can't be bought or sold. The knowledge you obtain can give you an advantage and cheat code that no one else has. Millionaires feed their minds daily because they understand you are not a student of life. You should never feel so well off that you can't learn anything else. No one is truly a master in

this world because we continue to learn new lessons as we reach new levels.

GOOGLE A LIST OF BOOKS TO READ.
WRITE THEM DOWN ON THIS PAGE.

Life is short.

Make sure you spend it with people who make you laugh, love, and care about you.

People get caught up in the "I don't need anyone" mentality. When in reality, everyone needs someone. In my life, I have been to jail over 20 times, and I have been shot as well. When you go to jail, you think those people you showed love to will do the same. In my case, that wasn't the case. People I fed, looked out for, and showed the utmost respect and love to turn on me. I would give the clothes off my back to walk bare for someone I love so as not to get that love in return hurt. The thing that we have to realize is that not everybody loves us. Not everyone has a sense of loyalty. Some people are leeches. Simple as that.

You never change who you are; you remove yourself and be around the people who reciprocate your energy. Some people get depressed because they don't receive what they put out from others. We have to remember that everyone has free will. That means we have a choice to do whatever it is we want to do. Also, remember that no one will be 100% like you. It's hard to swallow, but it's the world's reality. When I got shot, I didn't have many people willing to help me recover as I thought. I would move mountains and stop anything to help anyone I love who was physically, mentally, or spiritually ill. Again everyone isn't like me.

Through these experiences, I learned not to complain but to be around those who

love as I do. I learned to be around those with the same morals, values, and

integrity as I do. Once I realized that I have been around genuine love ever since.

WHO DO YOU ENJOY SPENDING TIME WITH AND WHY?

This week will be better for you.

Believe it, see it and work hard for it.

Mondays are days that most people hate. I think it's because we aren't happy with our jobs; therefore, we are programmed to hate the beginning of the week and love the end when we break from it. Your mindset is key to a great week. You'll be miserable every Monday if you go in hating Mondays and counting down until Fridays. However, if you shift your mindset and realize that each week brings new opportunities, you won't hate Mondays; you'll look forward to it. If you hate the beginning of the week because of your job, here's some advice: get a new one. Life is too short to be miserable, slaving in a workplace that will replace you if you die tomorrow.

There's no secret that we need income for the basic needs of life. But nowhere does it say you have to be miserable while doing it. Everyone isn't meant to be a business owner; not everybody desires that, and that's okay. There are millions of entry-level high paying jobs that you can get and be happy while doing it. Leveling up doesn't always have to do with business. You can level up working for a great company as well. Whatever your dream is, a new week is a fresh start to attack that dream.

This book isn't just for people who are business owners. This is for anyone who needs the motivation to keep pursuing their goals. Work hard for that new job promotion, get that new good-paying job, and work hard for that business. Remember, a new week equals new money and new opportunities.

WHAT CAN YOU DO TO MAKE THIS WEEK BETTER THAN LAST WEEK?

One day you will become everything you wanted to be.

This is one of the most important quotes in this book. Why? Because you must understand that despite the struggle, worry, anxiety, and stress, if you keep going, you will be everything you dreamed of and more. One day all the money problems, life circumstances, dead-end jobs, and fake friends will be a distant memory. You can reflect on those things while sitting around and enjoying the fruits of your labor. I keep saying it, but the most important lesson is not giving up.

You'll be able to write a book just as I did, detailing some experiences so that you can inspire the people who are watching you and coming up after you. We can finally break generational curses and teach our kids the blueprint. I want you to write your 3-, 6- and 9-month goals on paper. These are called short-term goals. As you complete them, scratch them off and move on. Write down your 1-year, 5-year, and 10-year goals on a separate paper. These are called long-term goals. Never lose this paper because you can reflect on your goals and realize how far you have come.

When you reach the level you envision, make sure you start over and journal your experiences, getting to the success you wanted. You can always give those journals to your child or anyone you inspire. That way, they too can use it as a motivational aspect in their life. We all need a little motivation for someone from time to time.

Don't forget to give them a copy of this one as well.

WHO DO YOU WANT TO BE?

No matter how you feel

in your journey, never settle for less.

Often we forget who we are while going through a period of change. When becoming a business owner or finding out which career we want, sometimes we feel less than others. To get to where you are going, you must believe in who you are despite your circumstances. I don't care if you are homeless; remember who you are and where you are going. This goes back to mindset.

Never settle for anything less than what you feel you deserve. In my eyes, all that matters is that you know your worth. Here's an example. You get a $20,000 brand deal with a major company. You have done the work and calculations and know that your brand is worth $800,000. Here it gets hard; you have overdue bills, your car just broke down, and you have kids to take care of. In your mind, this is a complete payday. You need this money to get you out of a financial bind. So what do you do? Do you settle for the 20K or decline the offer? Here's what I would do.

I would decline the offer. I know my and my company's worth; therefore, I would never let anyone play me. Once you know your worth, you won't settle for anything. I don't care what situation I am in; I would never let it forget who I am.

Don't let anything make you forget, either. Don't take any dollar amount because the next deal could be 2 million.

HOW DO YOU TRULY FEEL ABOUT YOURSELF?

Stay pure because with a pure heart

you will have longevity in life.

There is no secret that this world is wicked, damaged, and needs a deep cleanse. In a world like this, we must remain pure and remember to be true to ourselves just because people around us do devious things that don't make it right. I believe that as long as you stay pure, the blessings will always come, and you will live a long life. Karma doesn't skip anyone, so the minute that heart changes, you start doing other dirty things. Remember, it's coming back to you full circle.

There are a lot of people who will do anything to reach the top, and that includes stepping on or running over other people. That's not something I stand on. I see that it's becoming very popular on social media as well. People glorify messing over others and think those rewards will be long-term. It won't. You don't get blessed when you do things to people who don't deserve it. You don't get blessed when you kick others down to reach your potential. In the end, I promise you will get your karma somehow. What goes around truly comes around, and that's a proven fact. How you start is how you will end. So make sure you be careful how you treat other people in situations because you'll be on the other end sooner than you think.

HOW CAN YOU MAKE A POSITIVE
EFFECT ON SOMEONE'S LIFE?

Always trust your product.

When creating a product, brand, or business, you must trust what you are making. It's simple if you don't trust it, then who will? This ties into believing in yourself, manifestation, and positive energy. If you create anything and do it with doubt and negative energy, the outcome may be something you don't want. When we do things, they have to be with a pure heart and conscience so we can get the best results. Yes, hard work and dedication play a huge part in things but so does your mental state.

Now I'm not saying you can't create overnight success because with God, anything is possible, but it isn't common. And sometimes, people believe that their product isn't worth it because they didn't achieve this rapid success. This isn't realistic. Despite not generating overnight success, that doesn't mean your product isn't worth it. That doesn't mean it isn't a good product that people don't need. It means you continue to trust your product and be patient because your time is coming.

I don't care if you get one sale a month starting; never not trust what you have in front of you. Even if you feel like the market is over-saturated, remember there are 15-20 vegetable, meats, bread, and food companies selling the same thing in one store and still generating millions. What's for you will always be for you. Trust

your intuition and trust whatever it is you are creating.

WHY DO YOU TRUST YOUR PRODUCT? WHAT BENEFIT DOES IT HAVE FOR YOUR CUSTOMERS?

Remove yourself immediately from toxic relationships.

For some people, this can be the hardest thing to do, and some people have a hard time letting go of toxic relationships because of love, convenience, or even the time they put in. Toxic relationships only damage us in the long run. People glorify toxicity on social media because they think it's cute but forget the definition of toxic. According to the dictionary, Toxic means about, affected with or caused by a toxin or poison. When I think of the word poison, I think of something deadly and dangerous that will decline my health. Why would you want someone around you like that?

Toxic relationships can be deadly, and here's how, it can kill dreams, motivation, hope, self-love, and most importantly you. Once social media started glorifying toxic traits and throwing the word around, it became something cute and not taken as seriously as it should have. Toxic is toxic no matter how you dress it up and change the narrative of the original origin. My question to you is, are these relationships worth you? This can be any relationship, whether romantic, platonic, or family. Is it worth killing something attached to you?

The answer for me will always be no. Why would my life, goals, dreams, and plans be worth more than someone else? Why would I be less important than the person causing me harm?

This also goes into self-love. Because with self-love, you won't allow a toxic situation to get that close where they can poison what you have going on. Someone with self-love would leave immediately because they know their worth. They know what's at stake when dealing with poison and understand the damage it can cause. This is one of the most important quotes because our Queens and Kings have lost their lives due to toxic situations and not leaving before it's too late. If anyone reading this is in a toxic situation, I hope you realize how special you truly are and leave immediately before the poison does its job.

IF YOU ARE IN A TOXIC SITUATION OR
RELATIONSHIP, HOW WILL YOU
IMMEDIATELY REMOVE YOURSELF?

Seek help when life is too much to bear.

(Men)

As we all know, mental health is more important than ever today. I want to address the men because although this affects our Queens, I think men are less likely to go and get help. We, as men, have all been told that crying isn't okay. We've been told that if we don't look a certain way, dress a certain and don't have a certain amount of money in our pocket; then we aren't worthy. We walk around every day in fear that if a police officer stops us that it can be our last walk because of our skin color. We are told that when we get depressed, sad, or feel like we need help, we are weak. They tell us to man up and handle it. But when is enough enough? When do we realize that we are human? We aren't robots. We have feelings and are entitled to feel sad, weak, or depressed. We are entitled to feel emotions. We are also entitled to help. It is not weak if you need to speak to a therapist.

Get the help you need because the suicide rate is higher in men than in women. We will take the after-life road not to be judged because we need help. I'm here to tell you, King, you are not weak. Please get help because someone loves you and needs you in this world. There is someone you are impacting and don't even know. Your light shines bright like anyone else's.

To the Kings that are single fathers, I don't think you get the acknowledgment as much as you should. You work, take care of your kids, cook, and then handle life on your shoulders while battling your thoughts. You aren't weak. I stand with you. Please seek help to teach your sons and daughters that it is okay to get help. You are who they look up to and need. Never forget that.

If you Kings don't take anything from this book, I want you to please take your mental health seriously. I don't care if you work at McDonald's; you are worth it. You are making a living, and you are doing it legally. Never let anyone make you feel bad about your situation because they are on the outside looking in. Take self-care days as well, just like our Queens. Have you some time? Take a bath, sit on what you like, and do something you love, just like our Queens. You aren't feminine; you aren't anything but a man loving himself through life. Life is hard enough, so make it easier knowing you deserve all the love and support you can get.

Taraji P Henson offers free men's therapy at: borislhensonfoundation.org

National Suicide Prevention Line: 1-800-273-TALK

If you have health insurance, google therapist in your area. As a man, I stand with you. My love and support are forever with you

HOW IS YOUR MENTAL HEALTH? WHAT STEPS HAVE YOU'VE TAKEN TO IMPROVE THE WAY YOU FEEL?

Seek help when life is too much to bear.

(Women)

Queens, it's your turn. I understand that you take care of the household. You cook, clean, mother, nurture, work long hours, and then come home and forget about yourself. You take care of everyone else's needs but your own. Why are you always last? Why are you always loving on everyone and forgetting yourself? As a woman, you are one of the strongest and most powerful forces, with God first. You can make a house a home. Groceries a meal and a broken man into a whole man. I am not saying it's your job to fix anybody but let's face it, some do.

You are natural healers and can take some simple ingredients and heal a cold. You know what to say when anyone's day is bad, and you light up every room. But let me ask, who lights your light when burned out? When life gets tough, whose shoulder do you lean on?

You are not too weak, broken, or busy to seek help when you need someone to talk to. People are willing and ready to assist you in feeling like the true Queen you are. It's okay to feel sad, depressed and overwhelmed, but I need you not to stay there because we need you, just like we need men. It's okay not to be a superwoman all the time. It's okay to feel weak and cry. It is okay to take time for yourself and focus on what makes you happy. Because if you don't put yourself and your mental first, you will have nothing to give yourself or anyone else. Do this for you.

Get free help at: thehopeline.com

National Suicide Prevention Line: 1-800-273-TALK

If you have health insurance, google therapist in your area. As a man, I stand with you. My love and support are forever with you.

HOW IS YOUR MENTAL HEALTH? WHAT STEPS HAVE YOU'VE TAKEN TO IMPROVE THE WAY YOU FEEL?

Even your family members will tell you, you can't do it.

But I am here to tell you, you can.

Besides ourselves, some of our biggest criticism and hate come from our flesh and blood. I think this is one of the hardest pills to swallow for some people. We believe our family will be our biggest cheerleaders because we have this grand idea. From experience, I can say that it will be the opposite sometimes. Before a family or friend supports your idea, it will be a stranger. A stranger will see your product and believe in it before the people who know you will. In my opinion, I have two theories for this situation. My first one is that sometimes family can't see past the little girl they knew growing up. They can't fantom you making this incredible product, brand, or career from nothing. While sometimes, it's hate that they didn't think of it first. Instead of asking for a handout, you got it out of the mud and pushed through. Can you say the same for some family or friends?

Maybe you can and perhaps can't, but for the ones that can, jealousy of how far you came will blind your people. Instead of asking how they will say why her or why him? While I say, why not? Either way, keep working towards greatness.

People without support become some of the greatest businessmen and women. It's not about where you are going and who approval you need along the way. It's about never giving up because you and I know the right approval is always on its way. Don't worry about them; they will come around, and if they don't, it isn't your loss; it's theirs.

WHAT IS THE BIGGEST OBSTACLE YOU NEED TO OVERCOME? WHAT STEPS CAN YOU TAKE TO OVERCOME IT?

Don't mix money and business with your friendships.

Most likely, it will ruin your friendships.

These are my opinions and are not always the case for everyone. I can say that I have seen people cross their day ones that they have been friends with for 20 years over a green piece of paper. Not every idea causes you to go into business with a friend. Some of yall want to take everyone with you on your blessing, and it backfires. Not every friendship is about making money together. You do not have to put everyone on to be a real friend. I don't care what social media says.

Everyone is not built to be a business owner or do business with you. Most people believe in splitting 50/50 of the company's earnings; I can't understand it. If you have a 50/50 partnership, who is the decision maker when neither of you agrees? See, if you tell a friend let's go into business, ill be 51% and 49%, some will feel that because yall are friends, you are playing them. There are NO personal feelings in business. There's no place for it. It will crash the business before it even reaches its fullest potential.

It's okay to keep friends just as friends and business associates as business associates. I don't understand where this friend has to be an owner because my mentality came from.

Yes, you can put your friends on; sometimes, it works out great. But from experience, I have seen it crumble people. These two things should always be separate unless you have a solid contract with separate lawyers. Everyone involved should understand that when we clock in for our business, we no longer engage as friends. We are business partners, and the friendship is left at the door. That doesn't mean back door or cut business partners out deals. Always do business with integrity. What it means is right now, I am not your best friend; we are running a company, so what I say shouldn't affect how we view each other when we leave. Many people won't get this concept, and some won't agree. That's okay; always do what works for you and your situation.

DO YOU BELIEVE IN MIXING FRIENDS
WITH BUSINESS? WHY OR WHY NOT?

Don't waste your time hanging with people who have no goals.

They will bring you down.

The company you keep truly matters when you are climbing your way to the top. When you have friends who encourage you to go to the club every weekend and waste your money, I guarantee you won't reach your fullest potential. We are who we hang out with. If you were against abusers, would you hand with one? Probably not because you aren't one. Would you hang with someone who does hardcore drugs while you don't? You wouldn't because you wouldn't want to be around that thing.

Naturally, we won't be around people who do serious things like abuse people or do drugs. Why? Because we don't trust those kinds of people. We don't trust them because we don't agree with their decisions. So why would you hang with someone who has no ambition in life? It seems small, but it's very big. A friend who doesn't have goals can sometimes make you think your goals aren't important. If you have a strong mind, you'll get tired of being around someone who doesn't align with your purpose. You'll get tired of always going out because you have things to accomplish. You have to watch the company you keep around you. You can be blocking your blessings just by your circle. Everyone is different, and I am not judging how they choose to live; watch whose in yours.

WHAT KIND OF VALUE DO THE PEOPLE
IN YOUR LIFE BRING YOU?

Never stress yourself about things you have no control over.

In life, we all go through things that cause us stress. They keep us up at night and sometimes cause serious health problems. Stress can kill you. That's as simple as I can put it. I know our world says we should all be taking classes on becoming an overnight millionaire, and we should all be business owners by now. They say we should all drive foreign cars and dress in a designer. Seeing and hearing this causes some of you to stress, overwork, and try to make a life that you don't know is real.

You are stressing out if you should pay for a vacation or rent to keep up with strangers. Overworking and stressing your body to buy clothes from designers to look like you made it to strangers. Listen up and listen well. Do not kill yourself trying to impress people who could care less if you lived or died.

Sometimes we stress about our bills and place of employment. If you can change it, change it; if not, give it to God. My favorite line is, "Did it kill you?" It will not kill you if you don't have bill money this month. You will get through it. We have to learn to accept things and move forward. Get on a payment plan, pay what you can and pray. Give it to God. Don't stress over things that you can't change. Is stressing over the light bill going to pay it? No. You will be stressed, and it will still be past due. I am not saying don't pay bills, but if you are trying and don't have it. Give it to God. Stressing won't do anything but harm you. I would rather live with a past-due bill than hurt my body while it's still past due. Stress causes heart attacks, strokes, depression, and anxiety. I don't know about you, but I won't be having a stroke over no bill. My life is worth more than that.

WHAT ARE 3 STRESSFUL THINGS YOU ARE DEALING WITH IN LIFE? HOW CAN YOU OVERCOME THESE STRESSFUL THINGS?

Always choose the things you love doing.

When it comes to your happiness, nothing matters but you. I don't care what anyone says. We tend to forget what makes us happy vs. what makes other people happy. If you love reading, then read. Who cares what anyone has to say? Life is way too short to walk around people pleasing. When you look up, you will have spent your whole life not doing what you love for the sake of others.

I don't know about you, but I want to be 90-plus years old and thankful for the life I love. For the things I did to make me happy. I want to be grateful for the life I experienced. I don't want to get old and think wow, I should've gone skydiving. I should've traveled more. I should have eaten that burger. If you want to travel, go. If no one is there to go, go alone; make sure you take safety precautions.

If you want to enjoy food, eat it! So what if everybody has a coke bottle figure? Do what you love, do what makes you smile. Everyone isn't meant to fit into the life that was chosen for them. Never let anyone stop you from doing what you love, and make sure you aren't stopping yourself, either.

Self-doubt can hinder us from doing some great things. Fear can also play a huge part in that. Would you be happy with how your life turned out if you died today?

If the answer is no, you have some things to work on. If the answer is yes, then keep doing what you love. Either way, it's all about you.

WHAT ARE YOU CURRENTLY DOING
THAT MAKE YOU HAPPY?

Get rid of bad habits.

I want you to start making the steps today.

We all develop bad habits in life. No one is perfect; even with this book, you still won't be perfect. But we can all agree that some bad habits can hinder your success. For example, you may have a bad shopping habit that's causing you not to save. We all know that saving in this economy is more than important. You don't have to stop shopping, but you can limit it to save for a rainy day. That's a light habit that's an easy fix.

Now for the more serious habits. Some have smoking, drug, or drinking habits. Addiction can cause us to spend money on things despite us having to spend our money on more important things. Once an addiction or bad habit becomes so bad that you neglect your necessities, it's time to cut that out immediately. No habit is worth ignoring yourself over.

Our habits start small, and before we know it, they grow into these big things that we can't get rid of or becomes too hard to leave alone. Remember that it takes 21 days to form a good or bad habit. So start your 21-day journey of riding yourself through whatever habits you have that are holding you back from reaching your

fullest potential.

WHAT ARE SOME BAD HABITS YOU WOULD LIKE TO CHANGE?

When you make decisions, stand by them.

Regret is a huge factor in life. We all experience it, but unfortunately, we may continue to. That's because we are human, and life has no rule book. Along with regret, I think some people forget to stand by their decisions. Rather, it was good or bad; you decided it was best for you. Stand by it. Don't backtrack because things didn't turn out as planned, or you're receiving backlash. You made it based on your emotional state at the time. Does it make it wrong? Not completely. We all think differently at different times. We process things differently during different periods of our life. Therefore, a decision you made at 18 you probably wouldn't make at 25. Still, stand by it because that's where you were at the time.

In decision-making, there is nothing wrong with acknowledging the good, bad and ugly. It's a part of life; sometimes, it can cost us way more than we think. It doesn't matter, though; stand by it. Always keep your chin up and head high. Learn from it, but don't let it keep you sucked into deep regret. Some things will have you wishing you had a time machine. I've been there; hell, still. But I don't live in the past. I stand on anything I have done and accept it, knowing I may not know any better. Yes, our decisions can affect those around us. Still, stand by it because you made that choice. Too often, we see people doing evil things and pushing them off as if it wasn't their fault when it was. No one has the power to make you do

anything but God. Please don't put it off on anyone else. Take your consequence,

big or small, like a grown-up, and learn from it.

WHAT DECISIONS HAVE YOU MADE THAT YOU REGRET? WHAT CAN YOU DO DIFFERENTLY?

Please process the information you take in and let it apply the way you need to see transformations.

Most people nowadays have all the answers and advice to give. It doesn't mean you have to take it and apply it directly to your life. It doesn't mean you have to use it at all. But if you do, make sure you are processing it first and that it can affect you in a good way if you do. Not everything is for everyone or pertains to you. I think we let opinions affect us way too much. Because that's what it is, opinions. Here's an example. Shark tank is a TV show on ABC that allows investors to decide if they want to invest in a product. Inventors and business owners travel worldwide to pitch their companies to see if they have a product worthy enough for partnership and the capital they need. Most times, the money is to take their business to the next level, and so is the partnership with these celebrity investors.

After watching the show, I have seen some businesses I would invest in turned down, and I have also witnessed some investors tear people down about their products. Upon seeing this, I saw those businesses make millions of dollars despite the negative criticism they have received. Of course, the platform plays a part in sales. However, what if those people took the negative opinions from the investors and gave up? These are experienced business investors who have made billions but are they not human? Can they be wrong about a product? The answer is Yes because I have saw it happen. This is why you need to be careful of the information you process. What is not meant for someone else doesn't mean it's not meant for you.

Now, you have good information that helps you, makes your company better, and you become better. Still, process that information and make sure it is worth applying. Often we are too eager to jump on things because of what a person of status is saying. They know we don't, but they can still be wrong. We are all human at the end of the day. Do what works for you.

WHAT IS SOME VALUABLE INFORMATION YOU'VE LEARNED IN LIFE?

Never take your freedom for granted.

I've shared some personal experiences, but this one hits home. For the last 6 years, I have been fighting not to be deported back to Haiti due to a revoked bond with immigration. While fighting this case, I hadn't appreciated freedom more until I was on the run. I constantly thought about leaving everything I built in the United States and being forced back to my country. It's hard coming from a country people deem poor and creating a life for yourself only for it to be snatched away— how our brothers and sisters are treated is inhumane and sickening. So, to imagine myself going back when God blessed me to leave caused anxiety. I have been to jail, as you know, and I always appreciate freedom more and more as I get older. I realize how important it is to be able to walk down the street.

Wake up in your bed in your house at the time you choose. Do you see how powerful that is? You are the leader of your life. But when it is taken from you, someone else is the leader of your life. We must be careful of the things and situations we put ourselves in. One wrong move, and someone could be telling us what time to eat every day. We could call our family and hope they pick up the phone. Freedom is becoming a luxury. It's something we feel entitled to, but when we look at the world today and even during slavery. Freedom is a luxury that shouldn't be taken lightly. Our ancestors didn't have the right to freedom. They were beaten for trying to be free. They were deprived of the bare minimum to survive. Our ancestors from the Atlantic Slave Trade stood strong so we could live; some couldn't handle the pain and suffering. Remember our history. Remember why we are free. Because according to the constitution, once you are in jail, you are no longer free and a legally enslaved person at this point. Whenever you think about doing anything to jeopardize your luxury, make sure you remember those who don't have it.

EXPLAIN TO ME WHY YOU DON'T TAKE YOUR FREEDOM FOR GRANTED?

Drugs and alcohol can ruin your road to success. Don't take the route of suppressing your feelings.

Don't be the old me.

For years and years, I've been battling with taking drugs and alcohol, but I never really knew the real reason why. See, I was having fun with my friends, not knowing it was damaging me in the long run. Behind that, I have suffered many losses and lost connections with family, money, and even myself. Yes, I'm blessed and fortunate to do almost everything I want. For whatever reason, I used to be depressed and sad, even when recording at the studio; I always felt like I needed a drink or took a pill to feel better. To write my rhymes, but it was a mind thing I had to learn to be stronger mentally.

Drugs and alcohol abuse are killing us rapidly and won't stop until we address the pain and why we are using it to cope. As a person who was in your shoes, I have been there. I know what it's like to be so sad you pick up a pill to numb the pain. Sometimes the pain becomes too much to bear. Listen to me, drugs and alcohol will destroy you if you let it. It will create another person, and you will be a shell of the person you once were. I know success is hard, people are hard, society is hard, and the pressure to make a name for yourself is even harder. But you have to stay strong. When you feel stressed, depressed, or sad, do something productive to take your mind away instead of indulging in poison. Better yet, talk with a therapist. In the other chapter, I mention the importance of seeking help. If you can't do a quick cold turkey, get some help. Many successful actors, actresses, singers, rappers, and even politicians have been on drugs and changed their lives. You aren't less than for needing help.

If you or someone you love suffers from addiction, contact:

Mental health, Substance Abuse, and Drug Abuse: 1-800-662-HELP

For Kids and Teens: 1-855-DRUG-FREE

WHAT STEPS ARE YOU TAKING TO OVERCOME ANY ADDICTION?
(IF APPLICABLE)

You can lose everything and get it back.

Just make sure you never lose yourself.

I saved the best for last. We've discussed achieving success, losing people during success, and even mental health. But I didn't mention that never lose yourself when you succeed. This world is artificial; many things you see aren't real. People have sold and lost their souls for a dollar to end up broke. Please don't do it. Stay true to who you are no matter how much you make and how less you make. It is better to live happy and broken life than to be rich and miserable.

When you get everything you have dreamed of, and let's say you lose it somehow. I know it won't but for motivational purposes, let's go with it. So, you lose everything and never lose yourself in return. Now, you can learn from your mistake, gain it back, and keep it this time. So many people believe a loss is the end of it all. A loss is a failure, and a failure is a lesson not to fail again. Instead of not staying true to who we were in the first place, we go into a shell of what we used to be all because of a mistake. Did you die from any mistake you made? The answer is NO because you're reading this book. My point is it's not that serious about losing who you are. Death is the only thing serious enough to lose yourself; at that point, your journey is over. If you still have air in your lungs and a beating heart, there is no reason why you can't re-do mistakes. I don't care how many times you fail and mess up. Analyze, do it again and learn from it. If you made 100K and lost it, you know how to make 100K and keep it. Why? Because you lost it and you won't make the same mistake again. Never lose you. Take a page from this book whenever you feel down, stressed, or want to give up. It will be here forever to motivate you and guide you through life. When you're done, please give it to your kids. They will have a blueprint.

HOW WILL YOU APPLY WHAT YOU JUST READ TO YOUR LIFE?

"I embrace my past decisions and I don't regret any of the lessons I have learned. They made me who I am today."

"When you've overcome the pain that life brings, you can overcome anything.

Remember that change isn't to be feared but to be embraced."

Made in the USA
Columbia, SC
25 July 2023